EXPLORE ENGLISH

T0321879

Student's Resource Book 3

Contents

About this book

This book is full of interesting texts for you to enjoy.

● You can read and discuss **stories**.

Hector the hippo wanted to play the cello more than anything else in the world.

Suddenly, he had a plan! 'That's it!' he thought. 'I know what I'll do. It's the best plan.'

● You can read **information** about people, places and animals.

Families all over Egypt celebrate with a festival called Sham En-Nessim.

Dolphins can swim very fast and like to leap out of the water. They roll from side to side.

● There are **poems** to read aloud, perform and enjoy.

A friend
I can talk with a friend
and walk with a friend
and share my umbrella in the rain.

This tells you there is something to **talk** about.

This tells you there is something to **think** about.

Enjoy the book!

Family and friends

Read about Lee Chan and his family. Talk about your family.

Hello! My name is Lee Chan. I would like to tell you about my family.

My father is a pilot and my mother is a teacher. My sister is older than I am. She is twelve years old. I am nine years old. My baby brother is six months old. He cries a lot when he is hungry!

This is a picture of my family. My sister's name is Sandy. My baby brother's name is Steven. My father's name is King Fai. My mother's name is Kelly.

Sandy and I like baking. I like eating chocolate cakes. My sister likes eating biscuits.

My grandmother and grandfather are visiting us. They love being in the garden. They like listening to the birds.

This is my baby brother, Steven. He is laughing. He likes playing with his toes.

My cousin and I like swimming. My cousin's name is Meg.

Here is a picture of me with my friends. We all go to the same school.

Families are all different. Talk about your family.

My neighbourhood

Talk about the picture. What can you see in your neighbourhood?

Talk about which of these places you have in your neighbourhood.

school

park

library

dentist

swimming pool

doctor's surgery

supermarket

toy shop

What places do you like to visit in your neighbourhood?

In the classroom

Look at the picture of some children who are working hard in class. Then read the poem about some children who are *not* working hard in class.

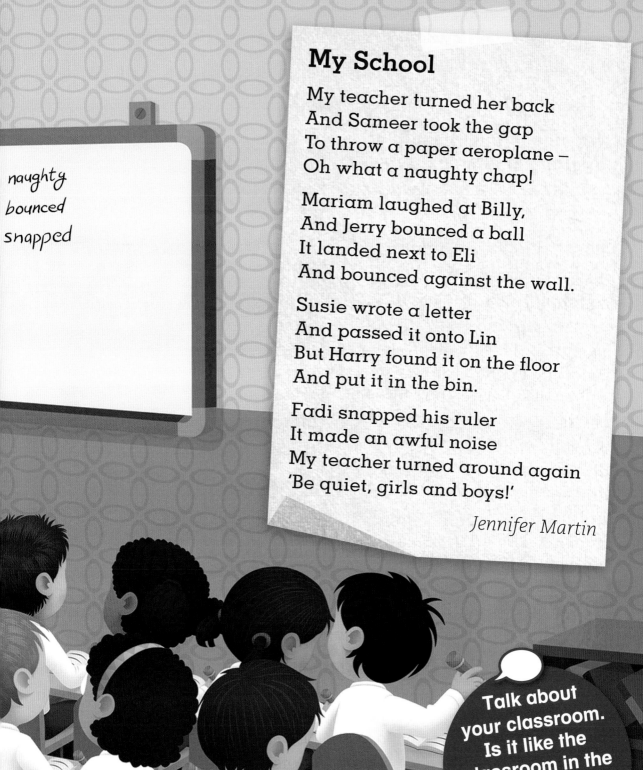

naughty
bounced
snapped

My School

My teacher turned her back
And Sameer took the gap
To throw a paper aeroplane –
Oh what a naughty chap!

Mariam laughed at Billy,
And Jerry bounced a ball
It landed next to Eli
And bounced against the wall.

Susie wrote a letter
And passed it onto Lin
But Harry found it on the floor
And put it in the bin.

Fadi snapped his ruler
It made an awful noise
My teacher turned around again
'Be quiet, girls and boys!'

Jennifer Martin

Talk about your classroom. Is it like the classroom in the picture, or is it like the classroom in the poem?

Celebrations

Read about four different celebrations around the world.

China

Chinese New Year is the most important celebration in the Chinese calendar. People wear red clothes. Children are given 'lucky money' in red envelopes and families eat delicious meals. Chinese New Year ends with a beautiful lantern festival and a dragon dance. Some dancing dragons are 100 m long! They are made of silk, paper and bamboo.

Thailand

Loy Krathong is Thailand's festival of lights. It takes place at the end of each year during a full moon. Families make a krathong. This is a small floating object filled with flowers and a candle. When it is dark, people float their krathongs on water. If your krathong floats away from you, it means you will have good luck for the next year.

Egypt

In Egypt, children have a day off school to celebrate the start of Spring. Families all over Egypt celebrate with a festival called Sham En-Nessim. The name of the festival means 'Smell the breeze' (breeze is another word for a soft wind). People go outside to parks and gardens to have a meal in the fresh air and enjoy the sunshine. They eat a special kind of fish with green onions and lettuce. They also decorate and eat eggs. The festival is thousands of years old.

What is your favourite special day in your country? Talk about the celebrations.

India

People in India celebrate a different festival of lights during Diwali each year. Diwali lasts for five days. Families decorate their homes with flowers and place small oil lamps called diyas, candles and coloured electric lights all around their houses. They also draw colourful rangoli, a pattern made in flower petals or rice flour, at the front door.

Party pictures

Look at the party pictures. Talk about what you can see.

What food do you like to eat at a party?

Which of these party ideas do you like?

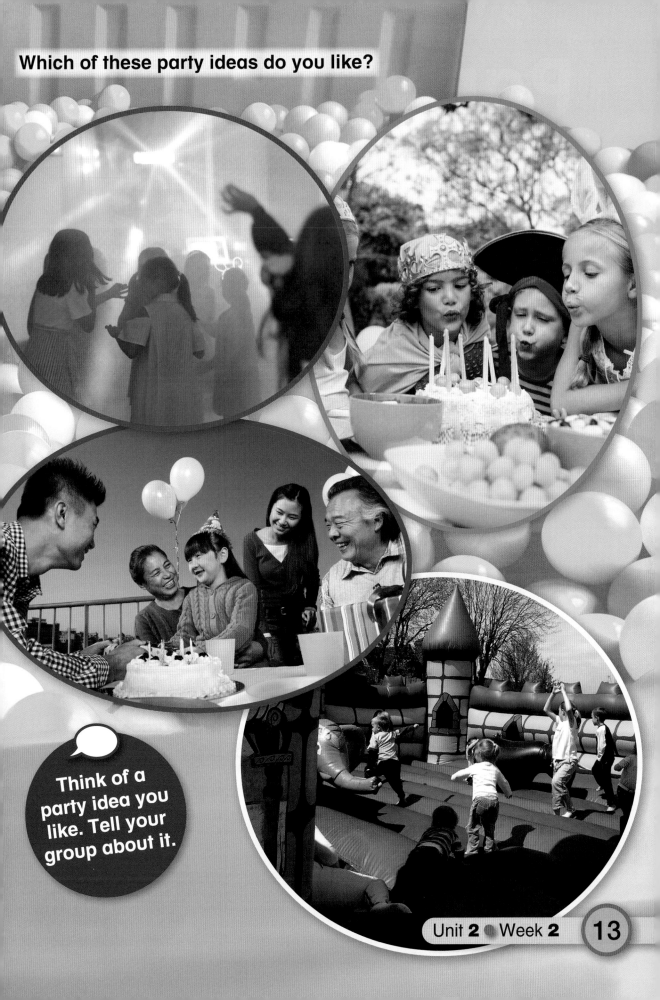

Think of a party idea you like. Tell your group about it.

Party snacks

It is important to follow recipes carefully. Read how to make these bright and colourful rainbow kebabs.

What you need:

- wooden skewers
- any type of washed fruit, such as apples, kiwis, grapefruit, strawberries, oranges, grapes, bananas and raspberries
- a small, sharp knife
- a small bowl

For the sauce:

- yoghurt and honey

Which fruit do you like? Can you use it to make party kebabs?

What you do:

1. Choose your fruit.
2. Rinse the fruit that will not be peeled.
3. Peel or remove the skin if you need to.
4. Cut the large fruit into bite-sized chunks.
5. If you have chosen oranges or grapefruit, separate the segments.
6. Small fruits, like strawberries, raspberries and grapes don't need to be cut.
7. Push the fruit chunks carefully onto the wooden skewers, in any order you like.
8. Then mix some yoghurt and honey in a little bowl … dip and eat!

Which recipe do you prefer? Kebabs or smoothies?

or … you can mix all the fruit, yoghurt and honey together and make a delicious smoothie.

Baby elephants

Read how the elephant centre cares for the baby elephants.

What happens to baby animals if their parents cannot look after them? Some orphaned elephants get looked after in an elephant rescue centre.

A baby elephant is called a calf. When a calf is born, it's nearly one metre tall! Elephant calves drink ten litres of milk a day for the first year of their lives.

The calves like their keepers at the elephant centre very much. It is important that different keepers look after the elephants because when a special keeper leaves the rescue centre, the elephants sometimes get sad and sick.

These baby elephants are drinking some milk.

Elephants are very clever. The keepers must keep them busy so they don't get bored. They take the baby elephants on long walks every day and also let them play with toys, like soccer balls!

When calves are two years old, the keepers move them to a national park where older orphan elephants live safely in the wild. The calves learn to use their trunks to get and eat plants.

The calves only spend time with the wild orphans during the day. At night they get looked after by keepers.

Elephants are very special animals. They never forget! Sometimes, when they are older, they come back to the rescue centre for help if they're hungry or hurt. Some elephants have even come to show keepers when they have a calf of their own! How do you think the keepers feel when this happens?

What happens when no one looks after animal orphans? Do you think it is important to help animal orphans?

Dreaming of dolphins

How much do you know about dolphins? Look at the photographs and read the information about swimming with dolphins.

Did you know that in some places you can swim in the ocean with wild dolphins? To do this, you must use special equipment. You must wear a wetsuit, a mask and a snorkel, and fins. The equipment helps you stay safe and lets you breathe when your face is under the water.

snorkel   mask

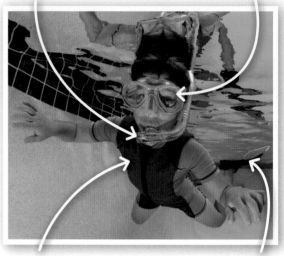

wetsuit   fins

Dolphins can swim very fast and like to leap out of the water. They roll from side to side.

They look very cute, and are often friendly and curious when they meet humans. Dolphins are wild animals and so people must respect the animals and their environment.

Do you want to swim with dolphins? Why? / Why not?

Important facts about dolphins

Dolphins live all over the world in seas and oceans. Some dolphins even live in rivers.

Dolphins eat fish, shrimps, squid and octopus. They hunt in groups.

Dolphins can swim up to 40 km per hour.

Dolphins call each other with clicking and squeaking sounds.

A male dolphin can live up to 30 years. A female dolphin can live up to 50 years.

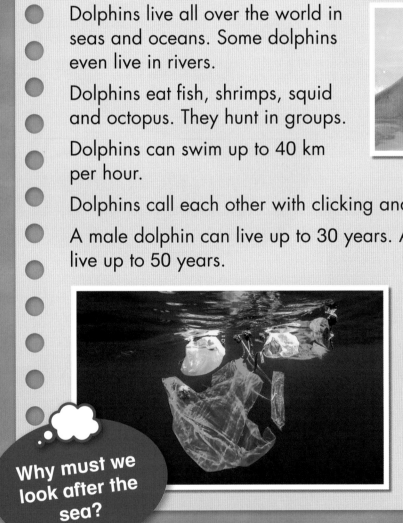

Dolphins must be protected.

We must look after our sea. We must not throw litter and plastic into rivers and the oceans.

We must also stop overfishing.

Why must we look after the sea?

Brown Bear and Wilbur Wolf

Look at the pictures. Then listen and follow the story about Brown Bear and Wilbur Wolf.

5

bear   mountain
beaver   river
deer   scared
forest   wolf
long

6

7

8

Can a wolf and a bear be friends? What other animals can become friends? Why?

The world of birds

Read the information about birds.

You can see birds all around you. Look for them flying around in parks and gardens and at the beach.

Seagulls have a loud screeching call. They eat things like fish, crabs and prawns.

All birds have feathers, but not all birds can fly. An ostrich cannot fly, but it can run very fast. It is the biggest bird of all. It is taller than a person.

Woodpeckers tap their beaks on tree trunks and make a loud rat-a-tat sound. They are looking for insects to eat.

Owls hunt at night. They can see in the dark and have strong beaks and sharp claws. Owls do not make any noise when they fly.

Do you know any birds that live in very cold or very hot places?

Parrots come from the Amazon rainforest. Some are red, yellow, blue or green. Some people keep parrots as pets. You can teach them to talk!

Do you want to do this?

Look at the photographs. Read the information and think about the questions.

We fly up to a height of 4,750 metres and then we open the door to jump. There is a rush of cold air when we open the door and during the first part of your jump. Most people are so excited they don't notice the cold at all.

Do you want to jump out of an aeroplane?

You free-fall for about 60 seconds before you open your parachute. But don't worry – you don't feel like you are falling at all. Free-falling is more like floating on a fluffy bed of air – you have to skydive to experience it!

Do you want to free-fall?

Some skydivers hold onto each other as they free-fall. They use a special grip to hold hands. This type of skydiving is also called bellyflying. Groups of four, eight and sixteen skydivers often take part in special competitions. The teams get points for style and how well they stay together as they free-fall.

Do you want to hold hands in the sky?

When you open your parachute, you slow down quite quickly. You must steer the parachute to make sure you land safely. Then you lift up your feet and slide to a stop. Someone on the ground helps you unhook the parachute.

Which do you think is more dangerous: swimming with dolphins or skydiving? Why?

Do you want to land like this?

Fly facts

You must have seen flies before, but how much do you really know about them?

Look at these pages from a website.
Read the information about flies.

| FIND OUT ABOUT FLIES | HOUSEFLIES | FLY FACTS |

FLIES

Did you know? Most flying insects have four wings. Flies only have two, but they are fantastic flyers. They can fly up and down, sideways and even backwards. They can also hover and spin – you'll know this if you've ever tried to catch a fly!

HOUSEFLIES

There are more than 120,000 types of flies. The dark grey flies found around where we live are called houseflies. (The green and blue flies are called bottle flies.) Adult houseflies grow to a length of 7–10 millimetres. They only live for 15 to 25 days.

Colour: Dark grey to black

Shape: Oval

Length: 5–7 mm

Legs: 6

Wings: 2 only

Female flies lay 500–600 eggs in their short lives. Baby flies are called maggots – they look like little fat white worms. The maggots will change into flies after about two weeks.

DID YOU KNOW?

Doctors can use maggots to help people with serious wounds and burns. They put the maggots onto the wound and they eat all the damaged flesh. This helps the wound heal. Maggots don't eat healthy flesh at all.

FLY FACTS
Where do flies live?

Flies live all over the world. They are found in hot and cold places.

HOW DO FLIES EAT?

First of all, flies taste food with their feet! When they land on food, they know immediately if it's going to taste good or not. Their feet are 10 million times more sensitive to sweet tastes than your tongue.

Flies don't have teeth so they can't bite or chew. Their tongues work like sponges to soak up liquids. When a fly lands on solid food it spits or vomits onto the food to make it into a liquid that it can soak up. Flies love any wet and rotten food, especially things with a strong smell.

DO FLIES SPREAD GERMS?

One fly can carry over a million different kinds of germs. That's a lot of germs! Flies have hairs on their legs and sticky pads on their feet. Germs and small pieces of things the fly lands on get stuck to the hairs and pads. Flies rub their legs together to clean them and the small pieces fall off – sometimes onto your food or your skin! Germs on their feet spread when they walk on different surfaces.

ARE FLIES HELPFUL?

You already know that maggots can be used to help clean wounds. Flies also provide food for many other animals including spiders, frogs, fish and chameleons. They also help to recycle natural waste such as dead animals and dung. So, although flies are a pest and they spread germs, they also have their uses.

Too Hot to Stop!

Listen to the story of Hoppitt the Gazelle and his friends.

In the desert in the east where the sand is so hot,

Hoppitt the Gazelle likes to hop, hop, hop!

Come and meet his friends in the desert sun.

Hop along with Hoppitt, the day has just begun!

The sand cat sat by the cactus tree.

'Come on, sand cat, come with me!'

The camel is a mammal with a hump upon his back.

'Follow us!' said the sand cat. 'Follow our track.'

'What's the hurry, Hoppitt?' asked the lizard in the shade.

'Come along, little lizard, join our parade.'

'Won't you stop it, Hoppitt?' said the fox on the rocks.

'It's too hot to stop,' said Hoppitt to the fox.

'Too hot to stop!' said the camel and the cat.

'Too hot to stop!' said the lizard at the back.

'Sss-stop it, Hoppitt, sss-stop it,' hissed the snake on a dune.
'If you're hopping up there, you'd better stop soon.'
'Stop it, Hoppitt, stop it,' warned the falcon, flying by.
'I can see where you're heading, from high up in the sky.'
Hoppitt hopped up the sand dune, so tall and so wide.
When he got to the top, he hopped off the other side ...
SPLASH!

A lake full of water, so deep and so cool,
Hoppitt splashed down into the desert pool.
SPLOOSH! came the camel, the lizard, snake and cat,
The falcon and the fox, with a SPLISH, SPLOSH, SPLAT!
'At last ...' said Hoppitt.
'This is where we stop it.'

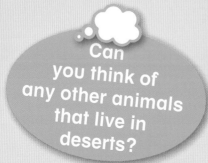

Can you think of any other animals that live in deserts?

Rally Challenge

Have you ever heard of rally car racing? Read this article about a rally car race.

Rallying is a type of motorsport. A rally is a car race that takes place on public and private roads.

The Dunlop Targa Rally takes place in New Zealand over six days. The cars all start the race at different times, and the car that finishes each stage in the shortest time is the stage winner. The car that is fastest overall wins the rally.

THE DUNLOP TARGA RALLY OF NEW ZEALAND

This is the route for the rally.

Auckland

New Plymouth

Hastings

Palmerston North

Wellington

— special stage
— touring stage

Each stage is a small race that is part of the main race. There are special stages and touring stages.

A special stage is a stage that takes place on roads that are closed to all other drivers. The rally drivers speed up on these stages because they don't have to worry about crashing into other cars.

To get from one special stage to another, the rally drivers use roads that are open to the public. These are called touring stages and the rally drivers must obey all the rules of the road.

Is it right to hold rallies in towns and cities? Why? / Why not?

The coldest place on Earth

Read about life in Antarctica. As you read, think about how hard it must be for the animals who live there.

Antarctica is the coldest and the windiest place on Earth. Temperatures can drop to −89°C (−129°F). The ocean around Antarctica has larger waves and stronger winds than anywhere else on Earth. In winter it gets so cold that even the snow freezes. Trees and bushes cannot grow there.

Some scientists live in special camps in Antarctica, but there are no towns or cities.

However, Antarctica is home to many animals, including orcas, seals and penguins. Seals are the penguins' greatest enemy.

Penguins are well suited to life in Antarctica. They have waterproof feathers and a thick layer of fat beneath their skin to keep them warm. This fat layer is called blubber.

Penguins cannot fly but they can swim very well. Penguins have to be great swimmers and divers because they get all of their food from the sea. They use their wings to help them swim. King penguins feed on squid and fish. The smaller types of penguins feed mainly on krill, which are tiny creatures like shrimps.

King penguins lay only one egg, and look after the egg by balancing it on top of their feet. They do not build nests. A special pouch covers the egg and keeps it warm. The newborn chick lives safely inside the pouch. The chick has a thick coat of brown, fluffy feathers. The mother and father penguins take turns to look after their egg or chick.

Can you think of other animals that live in very cold places?

Moving around the Sun

Read about the planets in our Solar System.

Venus is the brightest planet that can be seen from Earth. Venus has an atmosphere of sulfuric acid. Winds on Venus are very strong and fast.

Our home, planet Earth, is a very beautiful place. From a distance, our planet looks like a big blue marble. Earth is the only planet that humans, animals and plants can live on. Many people believe it is the only place in our Solar System where there is any life.

Mars

Earth is one of the planets that moves around (orbits) our Sun. The Sun and the planets are called the Solar System.

Earth

Mars is also called the 'Red Planet' because it looks red when you view it through a telescope.

Mercury

Venus

Mercury is the closest planet to the Sun. It has no atmosphere, so there is no wind or rain there. The surface of Mercury is full of big holes called craters.

Saturn is surrounded by seven rings made of tiny pieces of rock and ice. You can see these rings from Earth through a telescope.

Neptune was visited by the spacecraft Voyager 2 on August 25, 1989.

Pluto

Neptune

Uranus

Saturn

Pluto is furthest from the Sun. It is so small it is called a 'dwarf planet'. Pluto is a dark and frozen place.

Jupiter

Uranus is four times the size of Earth. It looks blue-green through a telescope. There are also very strong winds blowing on Uranus.

Jupiter is the largest planet in our Solar System. Jupiter is a very stormy planet. The Great Red Spot on Jupiter is a massive storm that has gone on for over 300 years.

Earth has a moon which moves (orbits) around the earth. All the other planets except Venus and Mercury have moons too.

The word *solar* means having to do with the Sun. What do you think these things are: a solar-powered calculator, a solar water heater and a solar eclipse?

Let's Go to Mars!

Imagine travelling through the Solar System to Mars. What an exciting adventure! Read about things to do on Mars.

Are you ready for the trip of a lifetime?

Our spaceship

You travel in comfort and safety in the latest spaceship. Don't worry about space junk hitting the spaceship because our spaceship has an extra-light, extra-strong skin that can repair itself if space junk hits it.

It takes five months to reach Mars, but if you book a ticket for the super-fast *Mars Express*, you can get to Mars in just three months!

In-flight entertainment

Enjoy the in-flight entertainment, including:

floating toothpaste

breakfast in a bottle

weightless football

What to wear

Be cool on Mars!

Our spacesuits have a stretchy undersuit with zip front and water-cooling tubes to keep you at the right temperature. There is even a drink bag inside the suit!

A **helmet** with **headphones** and **microphones** so you can talk to your family on Earth.

A stretchy undersuit with zip front and water-cooling tubes to keep you at the right temperature.

An in-suit drink bag.

Note: If you want to phone home, you have to wait almost 25 minutes for the person back on Earth to hear you. So phone conversations can take a long time!

What will you tell your friends when you phone them from Mars?

What can you do on Mars?

Read about what you can do on Mars. Which activities will you do?

You can build sandcastles.

You can enter the dune buggy races.

You can set a land speed record in a sand yacht.

You can be blown about in gigantic sandstorms. Don't get blown away!

You can hunt for signs of water.

5

You can watch red sunsets in a pink sky. The Sun will look half as big as it does from Earth.

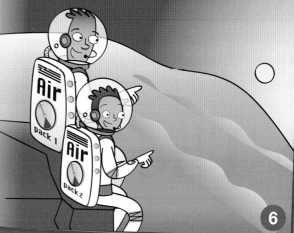

6

You can look for signs of life.

7

Life on Mars

You can have your photo taken under our sign.

8

Which activity on Mars will you do first? Why?

Space walk

If you look up at the night sky, you can see the Moon. Can you imagine walking on the Moon? Read this newspaper article about the first person to walk on the Moon.

The Daily Times

LATE EDITION   SUNDAY JULY 21, 1969

MAN MAKES IT TO THE MOON

Yesterday the astronaut Neil Armstrong stepped onto the Moon. He collected rock samples and planted the American flag before returning to his spaceship.

As he stepped onto the Moon, Neil Armstrong said, 'That's one small step for man, one giant leap for mankind.'

This footprint was made by one of the first astronauts to walk on the dusty surface of the Moon.

Imagine you are a reporter meeting the astronauts when they get back from the Moon. What questions will you ask them?

Space talk

Read about Galileo Galilei.

Galileo Galilei was born in Italy in 1564. He was an Italian scientist who studied the stars. At this time, people believed that the Earth was the most important part of the Solar System. They thought the Sun moved around the Earth.

Galileo did not agree – he believed that the planets moved around the Sun.

In 1609, Galileo invented the first telescope. A year later, he discovered that Jupiter had four moons, but nobody believed him.

In 1616, Galileo was not allowed to teach the idea that the Sun is at the centre of the Solar System anymore. Galileo was not allowed to leave his house and was not allowed to share his ideas.

Today we know he was right, after all.

Galileo with his telescope.

A modern space telescope.

How do you feel when no one believes what you say?

Hector and the Cello

Read this story about Hector, a very determined hippo.

Hector the hippo wanted to play the cello more than anything else in the world.

But who in the wild, wet jungle would teach him?

Hector tramped through the jungle to find a cello teacher. First he met a lion. 'I want to play the cello,' said Hector. 'Whoever heard of a hippo playing the cello?' roared the lion. He roared so loudly that his mane fell off. Hector picked up the lion's mane and draped it round his neck. It was going to be a chilly night in the wild, wet jungle.

On he tramped until … he met a leopard. 'I want to play the cello,' said Hector.

'Whoever heard of a hippo playing the cello?' growled the leopard. She growled so loudly that all her spots flew off. Hector picked up the spots and stuck them on his back. He might need a disguise in the wild, wet jungle.

On he tramped until … he met a rhino. 'I want to play the cello,' said Hector.

'Whoever heard of a hippo playing the cello?' snorted the rhino. He snorted so loudly that his horn fell off. Hector picked up the horn and went on his way. He could blow on the horn if he got lost.

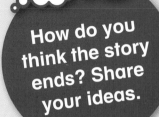

How do you think the story ends? Share your ideas.

On he tramped until … he met a slithery snake. 'I want to play the cello,' said Hector.

'SSSSSSSSSS. Hisssssssssss. SSSSTUPID! SSSSSILLY! SSSSAD!' hissed the snake. She hissed so much that she slithered out of her skin. Hector picked up the skin. He might need a cloth to wipe his cello in the wild, wet jungle.

On and on he tramped until … he met a lyrebird. 'I want to play the cello,' said Hector. 'Please don't roar, or growl, or snort, or hiss.'

'Do you have a cello?' asked the lyrebird.

'No,' said Hector. 'But I have a lion's mane, a leopard's spots, a rhino's horn and a snake's skin. Will that buy me a cello and some lessons?'

'Of course!' said the lyrebird, who was a good musician.

Every single day for two years, Hector tramped happily through the wild, wet jungle for his cello lessons.

Two years and one day later, there was a grand concert. All the animals from the jungle came.

Hector started to play. The sound was so sweet …

The lion roared for more.

The leopard growled with glee.
The rhino snorted with surprise.
The snake hissed with happiness.
So the musician gave the lion his mane back.
He gave the leopard her spots back.
… and the snake her skin.
He gave the rhino his horn …
In the wild, wet jungle the animals made music
until midnight.

What message does this story give?

The Brave Baby

1

Look at the pictures. They tell a story about a Chief and a baby who was not scared of him.

There was once a brave and fierce Chief. The people in the village were scared of him.

2

'Wasso, a little baby, is not scared of you,' said a wise woman. 'Look – she is playing with a stick.'

3

The Chief wanted Wasso to tell him why she was not afraid of him. Wasso began to cry. She would not go to the Chief!

Why do you think baby Wasso wasn't scared of the Chief?

The Chief tried to make Wasso stop crying. He danced a special dance.

Wasso liked the special dance – it made her happy, so she stopped crying. She soon fell asleep.

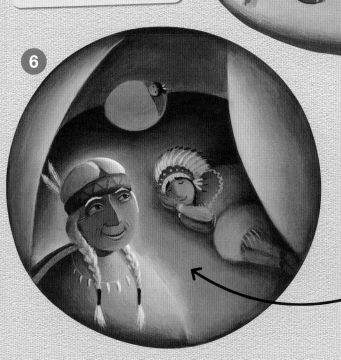

'You are right, Wise Woman, Wasso is not scared of me!' exclaimed the Chief. He was so tired from dancing that he also fell asleep!

Hansel and Gretel

A play script is written with different parts for each character in a play. This play has parts for seven characters. Work in groups of seven. Read the play aloud.

NARRATOR: Hansel and Gretel lived with their father and stepmother on the edge of a large forest. Their father, who was a very kind man, was worried. One day, he said to his wife (who was a very cruel woman) …

WOODCUTTER: What can we do? I need to feed my children, but I can't earn enough money.

STEPMOTHER: Well, you will have to do something. Why don't you send them away?

NARRATOR: The woodcutter and his wife argued all night. The next morning, the woodcutter walked slowly to where his children were sitting.

WOODCUTTER: Hansel, Gretel, come with me. We are going for a walk in the forest.

GRETEL: That will be fun. We will have a picnic there.

NARRATOR: Now Hansel, who had heard his parents arguing all night long, knew that they were not going to have a picnic. He was a very smart boy, and he hid a bread roll in his jacket pocket. Gretel chatted merrily to her father and Hansel walked behind them, throwing down crumbs along the way.

WOODCUTTER:	Let's stop here, children. Run along and play for a little while. I shall sit here and wait for you. You will have lots of fun playing in the forest.
NARRATOR:	When Hansel and Gretel returned, their father was gone.
GRETEL:	Oh no! What will happen to us? It is getting dark and I am scared.
HANSEL:	Don't be scared, Gretel. I dropped some crumbs on the path. We will look for them and they will guide us home.
NARRATOR:	Unfortunately, the birds had seen the crumbs and had eaten them up. Hansel who was a brave and a smart boy decided to find his own way home, but it became too dark to see and the children were soon lost.
GRETEL:	Hansel, I'm hungry and tired. Please let me rest for a little while.

NARRATOR:	Just then, the children saw lights twinkling in the distance. They ran quickly towards them, to see the most beautiful little cottage. The roof and the walls were decorated with sweets and biscuits and the curtains looked like candy floss! Hansel knocked carefully on the door.
OLD WOMAN:	Who is knocking at my door? One knock, two knocks, three knocks, four.
HANSEL:	Good evening, ma'am. Could you help us? My sister and I are lost.
OLD WOMAN:	Lost? Lost? That can't be true. Your family will look for you.
NARRATOR:	Hansel and Gretel were too tired to explain what had happened to them. The old woman invited them in.
OLD WOMAN:	Hahaha hee hee hee. Lovely children, just for me! I shall eat them, one by one, Yummy food inside my tum!
NARRATOR:	Hansel heard the old woman talking to herself. He whispered to Gretel…
HANSEL:	Gretel, that old lady is wicked. We must escape from here. We must run faster than the wind!
NARRATOR:	The old woman who was also a bit deaf was so busy stirring a stew in her cauldron that she did not hear the children creep carefully out of the house. They ran like the wind until they could no longer see the lights twinkling in the night sky. Hansel and Gretel were too tired to walk anymore and they fell asleep on the soft, soft grass under a

tree. The next morning, when they awoke, they thought they were dreaming, for there, sitting watch over them, was an owl.

OWL: Don't be scared. I will help you get back home safely. Just follow me.

NARRATOR: The children happily followed the owl, and before they knew it, they were back home again.

WOODCUTTER: Oh my children, I am so happy to see you! I have been looking all over for you! Come inside at once!

NARRATOR: The woodcutter had changed his mind about leaving his children in the forest, but when he reached the place where he had first left Hansel and Gretel, they were nowhere to be seen. He had spent the whole night looking anxiously for them. The stepmother was so surprised and angry to see Hansel and Gretel that she stormed off into the forest, never to be seen again. As for the woodcutter and his children, they lived happily ever after.

What fairy tales do you know from your country?

Look, but don't touch!

Read about some dangerous but wonderful sea animals.

The sea can be dangerous for humans, but it is also dangerous for some of the animals that live beneath the waves. Just like land animals, sea animals protect themselves.

Look at this triggerfish. It has a sharp spine on its head. Ouch!

This sting ray stays safe because it is electric. When you touch it you get an electric shock. So, don't touch!

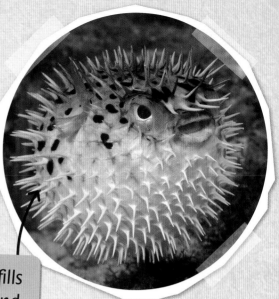

The porcupine fish has spines, too. It fills with water when it feels threatened and looks like a big spiky ball. Do you want to play with it?

Eek! Did you know you get snakes in the sea? This sea snake has teeth called 'fangs'. Its bite is poisonous.

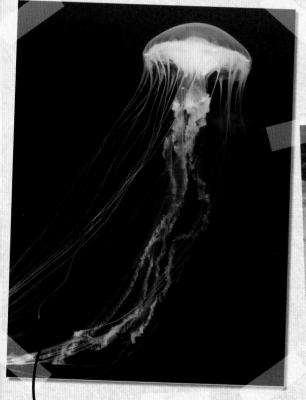

Jellyfish can sting you with their long, poisonous tentacles.

What other dangerous but wonderful sea animals do you know about?

Crocodiles and monitor lizards

Crocodiles and lizards have lived on Earth for millions of years. Look at the photographs and read about these animals.

Crocodiles

Large crocodiles only need a few big meals a year. The rest of the time they mostly eat fish.

Crocodiles are some of the best hunters in the world. They sneak up on their prey. Crocodiles grab their prey with their powerful jaws. They can snap their jaws shut with enough power to crush a car door.

Crocodiles catch their prey and try to drown it by pulling it underwater. Crocodiles have a flap of skin to stop water going down their throats, so they can go underwater with their mouths open.

Which animal do you think is more dangerous: a shark or a crocodile? Why?

Monitor lizards

Monitor lizards look a bit like crocodiles. Their mouths contain poison, and even if their prey escapes, it will often die later from blood poisoning.

Monitor lizards are scavengers. They eat anything they can find. They eat fish, dead animals, birds, frogs and other small animals.

Baby monitor lizards often live in trees, where they are safe from adult lizards who even eat baby lizards.

But like crocodiles, once they become adults, they are clever predators.

What other predators can you think of?

Big, bigger, the biggest

The three biggest animals in Africa are called 'The Big Three'. Read the information to learn more about them.

The huge African savannah is made up of grassland and some woodland. It's home to three of the largest animals on Earth: elephants, rhinos and hippos.

Elephants are the biggest of The Big Three.

An adult elephant can weigh 6,300 kg. How much do three elephants weigh?

Hippos are smaller than elephants and live on the banks of rivers and lakes.

Rhinos are also smaller than elephants but they can be as big as trucks.

Poachers get a lot of money for elephant tusks and rhino horns. Think of ways to protect these animals from poachers.

The Big Three are all endangered animals. This means that we must protect them to make sure they can survive in the future.

Humans are the worst enemies of elephants, rhinos and hippos.

People kill elephants for their ivory tusks. They kill hippos for meat and oil, and rhinos for their horns.

Game wardens try to stop the poachers, but they still kill many animals. We must protect Africa's big three animals before they are all gone.

We need friends

A friend

I can talk with a friend
and walk with a friend
and share my umbrella in the rain.
I can play with a friend
and stay with a friend
and learn with a friend
and explain.
I can eat with a friend
and compete with a friend
and even sometimes disagree.
I can ride with a friend
and take pride with a friend.
A friend can mean so much to me!

by Vivian Gouled

What do you do *with* your friends?
What do you do *without* your friends?
What do you do *for* your friends?

People who annoy us

Mark's Great Plan

Mark walked slowly home from school. He was hungry - again! An older boy in his school had taken his lunch again, and said that he would hurt him if he told anyone. Mark was very angry, and he wanted to do something mean to the boy. He walked home, kicking a stone, trying to think up a brilliant plan to take revenge on this mean bully.

Suddenly, he had a plan! 'That's it!' he thought. 'I know what I'll do. It's the best plan.' He ran home quickly, thinking about how he could make his plan perfect.

The next day, Mark walked to school, excited. He spent the day waiting for lunch time, when he knew the older boy would come and take his lunch box. He felt brave, and ready to take on the bully.

What do you think Mark's great plan is? What would you do?

The bully came to him at lunch time. 'Give it to me,' he said, as he held out his hand for the lunch box. Mark didn't even try to stop him. The boy took out the sandwich and ate it in front of Mark. Suddenly, his face went red and his eyes started to water. His nose also went red and started to run. He shouted, 'Give me water!'

As Mark watched the bully, he thought about making the sandwich that morning. He had buttered the bread, put on the cheese and tomato, like he did every day. And then he put on a thick layer of hot and spicy chilli sauce.

The bully ran away to get some water. Mark smiled. 'I am not as big as that bully, but I stood up to him,' he thought. 'I had a super plan and it worked.'

After lunch, his teacher called him to her classroom.

'Mark, I understand that someone was bullying you and that you are angry. But it isn't a good idea to be mean because someone is mean to you. If this happens again, you should come and tell me.'

As he walked home, Mark thought about this. Perhaps the teacher was right?

What do you think of Mark's plan? Do you think it was the right thing to do?

How to get along

Bullies can hurt us in different ways. They can:

say the meanest things to us
grab our things
make fun of us
threaten us
hit or punch us
break our things
make us do things we don't
   want to do

call us the worst names
scare us
tease us
make us feel the saddest people
   around
embarrass us

How do bullies make us feel?

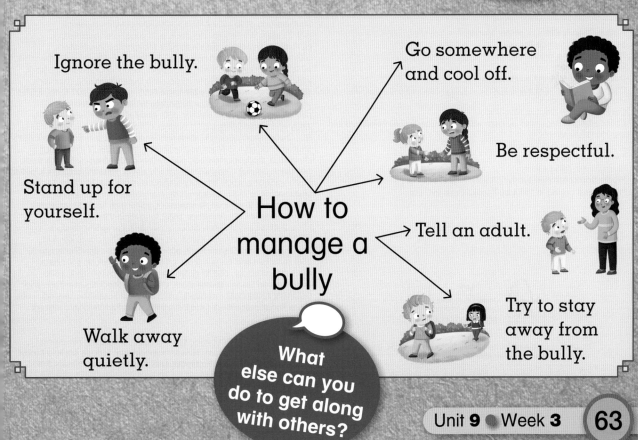

Ignore the bully.

Go somewhere and cool off.

Be respectful.

Stand up for yourself.

How to manage a bully

Tell an adult.

Walk away quietly.

Try to stay away from the bully.

What else can you do to get along with others?

William Collins' dream of knowledge for all began with the publication of his first book in 1819.
A self-educated mill worker, he not only enriched millions of lives, but also founded a flourishing publishing house. Today, staying true to this spirit, Collins books are packed with inspiration, innovation and practical expertise. They place you at the centre of a world of possibility and give you exactly what you need to explore it.

Collins. Freedom to teach.

An imprint of HarperCollins*Publishers*
The News Building
1 London Bridge Street
London SE1 9GF

HarperCollins*Publishers*
Macken House, 39/40
Mayor Street Upper,
Dublin 1, D01 C9W8,
Ireland

Browse the complete Collins catalogue at
www.collins.co.uk

© HarperCollins*Publishers* Limited 2021

10 9 8 7 6 5

ISBN 978-0-00-836912-5

British Library Cataloguing in Publication Data
A catalogue record for this publication is available from the British Library.

Authors: Sandy Gibbs, Jennifer Martin
Series editor: Daphne Paizee
Publisher: Elaine Higgleton
Product manager: Lucy Cooper
Development editor: Cait Hawkins
Project manager: Lucy Hobbs
Proofreader: Helen King
Cover design by Gordon MacGilp
Cover artwork: Reprinted by permission of HarperCollins Publishers Ltd © 2010 (Steve Webb)
Internal design: QBS Learning
Typesetting: QBS Learning
Illustrations: QBS Learning
Production controller: Lyndsey Rogers
Printed and bound in India by Replika Press Pvt. Ltd.

Acknowledgements
The publishers gratefully acknowledge the permissions granted to reproduce copyright material in the book. Every effort has been made to contact the holders of copyright material, but if any have been inadvertently overlooked, the Publisher will be pleased to make the necessary arrangements at the first opportunity.

HarperCollins*Publishers* Limited for extracts and artwork from:

Brown Bear and Wilbur Wolf by Sarah Parry, illustrated by Judy Musselle, text © 2012 Sarah Parry. *Fly Facts* by Janice Marriott, illustrated by Andy Keylock, text © 2004 Janice Marriott. *Too Hot to Stop!* by Stephen Webb, illustrated by Stephen Webb, text © 2010 Stephen Webb. *Let's Go To Mars!* by Janice Marriott, illustrated by Mark Ruffle, text © 2005 Janice Marriott. *Hector and the Cello* by Ros Asquith, illustrated by Ros Asquith, text © 2005 Ros Asquith. *The Brave Baby* by Malachy Doyle, illustrated by Richard Johnson, text © 2004 Malachy Doyle. *Hansel and Gretel* by Malachy Doyle, illustrated by Tim Archbold, text © 2006 Malachy Doyle.

Photo acknowledgements
The publishers wish to thank the following for permission to reproduce photographs. Every effort has been made to trace copyright holders and to obtain their permission for the use of copyright materials. The publishers will gladly receive any information enabling them to rectify any error or omission at the first opportunity.

(t = top, c = centre, b = bottom, r = right, l = left)

p7 (background) Inga Linder/Shutterstock, p10t Cora Reed/ Shutterstock, p10c testing/Shutterstock, p10b GOLFX/Shutterstock, p11t TasiPas/Shutterstock, p11b India Picture/Shutterstock, p11c Khaled Elfiqi/EPA-EFE/Shutterstock (also inset p3cl), p12-13 gui jun peng/ Shutterstock, p12t wavebreakmedia/Shutterstock, p12l Monkey Business Images/Shutterstock, p12b Sergey Novikov/Shutterstock, Yasemin Yurtman Candemir/Shutterstock, p13tl MakDill/Shutterstock, p13tr wavebreakmedia/Shutterstock, p13bl XiXinXing/Shutterstock, p13br Peter Baxter/Shutterstock, p14-15 paprika/Shutterstock, p14 Ozgur Coskun/ Shutterstock, p15 TUVISION/Shutterstock, p16-17 Jordi C/Shutterstock, p16t Barbara von Hoffmann/Alamy, p16bl Gary Roberts/REX/Shutterstock, p16br Gerry Ellis/ Minden Pictures/Getty, p17 Lisa Hoffner/naturepl, p18t Beth Swanson/Shutterstock, p18b Willyam Bradberry/Shutterstock (also inset p3b), p19t Paul Vinten/Shutterstock, p19c Steven Ramzy/ Shutterstock, p19b MOHAMED ABDULRAHEEM/Shutterstock, p22-23 Mark Winfrey/Shutterstock, p22t Juho Salo/Shutterstock, p22b paula french/Shutterstock, p23t Tobyphotos/Shutterstock, p23c duangnapa_b/Shutterstock, p23b Operation Shooting/Shutterstock, p24t Germanskydiver/Shutterstock, p24b Mauricio Graiki/Shutterstock, p25t Germanskydiver/Shutterstock, p25b Dreamframer/Shutterstock, p26t kurt_G/Shutterstock, p26b Latte Art/Shutterstock, p27 Cathy Keifer/ Shutterstock, p28 (background) Andrea Willmore/Shutterstock, p30-31 Andy and Angie Belcher, p30t Andy and Angie Belcher, p31b Andy and Angie Belcher, p31t Andrea Willmore/Shutterstock, p32-33 Li Hui Chen/Shutterstock, p32 vladsilver/Shutterstock, p33 Roger Clark ARPS/ Shutterstock, p34-35 Macrovector/Shutterstock, p36-37 (background) chonlathit_stock/Shutterstock, p38-39 (background esfera/Shutterstock, p40 (background) nienora/Shutterstock, p40bl neftali/Shutterstock, p40br Castleski/Shutterstock, p41tr iryna1/Shutterstock, p41bl Vadim Sadovski/ Shutterstock, p50-51 (background) Nearbirds/Shutterstock, p52-53 (background) GraphicsRF/Shutterstock, p54tr Rich Carey/Shutterstock, p54bl Vitaliy6447/Shutterstock, p55tl Jung Hsuan/Shutterstock, p55tr Beth Swanson/Shutterstock, p55br Rich Carey/Shutterstock, p55bl feathercollector/Shutterstock, p56-57 (background) komkrit Preechachanwate/Shutterstock, p56r Audrey Snider-Bell/Shutterstock, p56l Jonathan and Angela Scott, p57l E. O/Shutterstock, p57r Natali Glado/Shutterstock, p58-59 Galyna Andrushko/Shutterstock, p58b Donovan van Staden/Shutterstock, p59t Travel Stock/Shutterstock, p59c GUDKOV ANDREY/Shutterstock, p59b Svetlana Foote/Shutterstock, p60t Tinna Pong/Shutterstock (also inset p3b), p60b FamVeld/Shutterstock

With thanks to the following teachers and schools for reviewing materials in development: Hawar International School; Melissa Brobst, International School of Budapest; Niki Tzorzis, Pascal Primary School Lemessos.